Other titles in the BUSTED! series

Alcohol = Busted!
ISBN 0-7660-2552-7

Crack & Cocaine = Busted!
ISBN 0-7660-2169-6

Ecstasy = Busted!
ISBN 0-7660-2387-7

Heroin = Busted!
ISBN 0-7660-2386-9

Marijuana = Busted!
ISBN 0-7660-2550-0

Meth & Speed = Busted!
ISBN 0-7660-2551-9

Heroin =

Holly J. Hager

Enslow Publishers, Inc.

40 Industrial Road   PO Box 38
Box 398   Aldershot
Berkeley Heights, NJ 07922   Hants GU12 6BP
USA   UK

http://www.enslow.com

For Michael, Tommy, and their families.
May their suffering keep others from suffering.

Library of Congress Cataloging-in-Publication Data

Hager, Holly.
    Heroin=Busted! / Holly J. Hager.— 1st ed.
      p. cm. — (Busted!)
    Includes bibliographical references and index.
    ISBN 0-7660-2386-9
    1. Heroin habit—Juvenile literature. 2. Heroin—Juvenile literature. 3. Teenagers—Drug use—Juvenile literature. I. Title. II. Series.
    HV5822.H4H27 2005
    362.29'3—dc22   2004019267

Printed in the United States of America

10 9 8 7 6 5 4 3 2 1

To Our Readers: We have done our best to make sure all Internet Addresses in this book were active and appropriate when we went to press. However, the author and the publisher have no control over and assume no liability for the material available on those Internet sites or on other Web sites they may link to. Any comments or suggestions can be sent by e-mail to comments@enslow.com or to the address on the back cover.

Illustration Credits: Central Intelligence Agency, p. 15 (bottom); Corel Corporation, pp. 12–13, 24–25 (background); Digital Stock, pp. 10, 64–65, 69; Drug Enforcement Administration, p. 44 (all); Enslow Publishers, Inc., p. 38; © 2004 JupiterImages, p. 15 (top); Library of Congress, pp. 31, 36 (top and bottom); LifeArt, p. 18; National Archives, pp. 21, 24 (inset), 28, 33 (top and bottom), 59; National Institute on Drug Abuse, p. 17; stockbyte, pp. 6–7, 46–47, 72–73.

Cover Illustration: Digital Stock

CONTENTS

CHAPTER ONE

BUSTED

Ed was working undercover for the Houston police. He was targeting a drug dealer named Bobby T. In his early twenties, Bobby T. had already become a popular drug dealer in the nightclub scene.

Bobby T. had not finished school, and he did not have a job. He was making too much money selling drugs, and he was using too many drugs to think about his future.

Bobby T. thought he would never go to jail because of drugs. But Ed had other plans. Ed knew that the drugs Bobby T. was selling could kill him and others. If he had to put Bobby T. in prison to keep that from happening, he would.

Ed started going to the clubs where Bobby T. sold drugs. At first, Ed acted like he was just having a good time. Then he started buying drugs. He started out buying a little bit from people who worked for Bobby T. But eventually Ed worked his way up to buying the worst drug, heroin.

As Bobby T. got used to seeing him around, Ed started buying more and more heroin. Bobby T. thought Ed was just another heroin user, a junkie. He never thought Ed might really be a law enforcement officer who was building a case against him. Eventually, Bobby T. sold heroin directly to Ed.

Over several weeks, Ed bought enough heroin from Bobby T. to send him to prison for several years. Then one night, Ed came to one of Bobby T.'s clubs. Instead of buying more heroin, Ed arrested Bobby T.

Bobby T. went to prison for five years, and he lost everything his drug money had bought him.

* * *

Several years after Ed busted Bobby T., Ed was walking on the street when someone called his name. He turned around and saw someone who looked like a much healthier version of Bobby T. The bones in his face did not stick out anymore, and there were no dark shadows under his eyes.

As the new Bobby T. walked over to Ed, he wondered if Bobby T. was still as angry as he had been the night he was arrested. But Bobby T. looked anything but angry.

Bobby T. held out his hand for Ed to shake it and asked, "Hey, do you remember me? You arrested me."

Ed nodded and shook Bobby T.'s hand, still wondering if he would blame Ed for sending him to prison for five years of his life.

Bobby T. shook Ed's hand. "Thank you. You saved my life."[1]

Bobby T. was very lucky. Once someone starts using heroin, they normally begin a lifelong fight that ends when they lose everything, not just for five or ten years, but permanently.

Drug use and abuse lands people in jail.

Heroin is an incredibly dangerous drug. Heroin abuse usually leads to crime, financial ruin, and finally death. Heroin offers a total escape from reality. That is why most people first try heroin. They are looking for an escape from their problems. What they do not understand is that heroin will not just make them escape their problems; it will make them escape everything, including their friends, their families, the desire to eat or sleep, and often the ability of their heart to keep beating. After even just a few uses, heroin often makes people want to do nothing but use heroin until it kills them.

Although heroin is usually this destructive, in 2003, more than one in a hundred eighth-graders in the United States admitted to having tried heroin at least once.[2]

In 2003, over 15 percent of U.S. eighth-graders thought that heroin would be fairly easy or very easy for them to get.[3]

CHAPTER TWO

FROM FLOWER TO FATAL

Heroin is made from opium, and opium comes from the opium poppy plant (*Papaver somniferum*). Poppy plants take about three months to bloom. As the poppy flower dies, the petals fall off and leave an egg-shaped seedpod. The pod contains a milky white sap. This sap is the most basic form of opium.

Farmers harvest opium by cutting slits in the poppy pod with a curved knife. Cutting the pod lets the sap ooze out to form a brownish-black, gum. Farmers scrape this opium gum off the pods and combine it into larger balls, or cakes, that they then sell to a local refinery.

At the refinery, workers boil opium with chemicals like lime to purify it. Most of the mixture sinks to the bottom of the pot. Only a white band of morphine floats to the top. The morphine is skimmed off and mixed with ammonia before it is reheated. Then this mixture is filtered with activated charcoal and boiled again to reduce it to a brown paste, the morphine base.[1]

The brown paste is poured into molds and dried in the sun. This paste can be smoked to make the user feel "high." But heroin is a much more pure form of opium that is cooked and filtered several more times than morphine.[2] Because of its purity, heroin is the strongest and most deadly opiate.

Heroin can be smoked, snorted through the nose, or injected directly into a vein. Heroin users will risk the many dangers of injecting ("shooting up") heroin because they need to get the biggest

Farmers harvest opium by cutting slits into poppy pods (top).
Recently harvested opium gum (bottom) will be poured into
molds and dried in the sun.

- It takes about ten tons of raw opium to make one ton of heroin.[3]
- An addict may use heroin every four to six hours in doses of four to eight milligrams each.[4]

high that they can from the least amount of the drug.

But researchers have found that smoking, shooting up with, and snorting heroin give close to the same results. They all get heroin into the blood within one to two minutes. A low dose of heroin gets the user high within five to fifteen minutes. A large dose gets the user high in about two minutes.[5]

Heroin moves quickly from the blood to the brain. When it reaches the brain, the brain turns heroin into morphine. Morphine is a lot like another chemical that is naturally in the brain. This chemical is called an endorphin.

The body makes endorphins when it exercises or when it is under stress. Endorphins do two things. They make the body feel good, and they relieve pain. If someone is running around outside and feeling really good, his or her brain is swimming in endorphins.

Because it is important to feel good, the brain has special cells that are only there to absorb endorphins. When morphine gets into the brain, it acts just like an endorphin. Morphine goes right to the cells that absorb endorphins. These cells absorb any morphine (or the heroin that is converted into morphine) that comes into the brain.[6]

There is one big difference between endorphins and heroin. The brain only makes as many

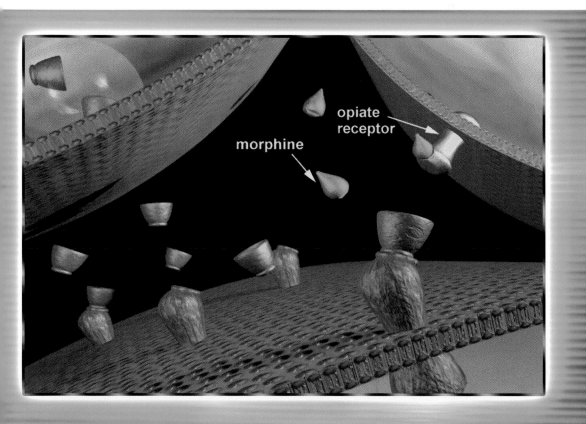

Morphine acts like endorphins in the brain.

Opiates Act on Many Places in the Brain and Nervous System

Opiates can change the brain stem, an area that controls automatic body functions, and depress breathing.

Opiates can change the limbic system, which controls emotions to increase feelings of pleasure.

Opiates can block pain messages transmitted by the spinal cord from the body.

endorphins as it needs. But when someone uses heroin, he or she decides how much to take. The more heroin someone uses, the more heroin the user needs to get the same effect. Eventually, if a heroin user does not take the drug, he will get sick. Heroin addicts usually take amounts of the drug that are much more than their bodies need or can handle.

The intensity of a heroin high depends on:
- how much heroin is taken
- how quickly it gets into the brain
- how quickly the brain absorbs it [9]

Over time, using heroin can actually change a person's brain and nerves. These organs control emotions, senses, and the way the rest of the body works.

Heroin blocks how much pain a person can feel. Stopping pain might seem like a good thing. But pain is the body's warning system. Nerves send out pain messages to let the brain know something is wrong with another part of the body. For example, the pain a person feels when he or she touches something hot makes the hand pull away before it can be burned. By stopping feelings of pain, heroin stops users from being able to protect themselves.[10]

Heroin can also change the way the brain controls automatic body functions. Automatic body functions are the things organs do without a person thinking about them—like breathing, heartbeat, and digestion.[11] These are the things that keep a person alive from minute to minute. The more pure heroin is, the more chance it has of disrupting a user's automatic body functions.

Pure heroin is a bitter-tasting powder.[12] But powdered street heroin is mixed ("cut") with other powders to make a bag of it look like more than it really is.

Street heroin is sold in five- and ten-dollar bags. The more heroin a dealer puts into each bag, the less money he makes on that bag. But dealers do not try to put as little heroin into a bag as possible because they want their customers to come back. The more pure heroin they put into each bag, the more money they will make in the long run by increasing the amount of heroin a

Heroin can be taken many different ways. Some users smoke it
in cigarettes. Heroin is deadly no matter how it is taken.

To keep addicts coming back, dealers will vary the amount of heroin they put in bags, balloons, or capsules.

user needs to get high. To keep addicts coming back, dealers usually vary the amount of pure heroin they put in each bag they sell.

The most common ways to cut heroin are to add powders that are not harmful to the body such as sugar, starch, or powdered milk. But street heroin can also be cut with powdered poisons that are harmful. Since heroin is illegal in the United States, no one controls its production. Heroin users can never know the strength or the real contents of the drugs they put in their bodies. They are always at high risk for taking more than their bodies can handle ("overdosing") or death.[13]

CHAPTER THREE

PUTTING OUT FIRES WITH GASOLINE

People around the world have been using opium for thousands of years to relieve pain and to stop bleeding. Although opium effectively relieves pain, it makes users so dreamy and sleepy that they do not want to do anything else. All they want to do is take more heroin.

- Euphoria
- Warm skin
- Dry mouth
- Heavy limbs

- Suppression of pain
- Irregular heartbeat
- Slipping back and forth from being alert to sleepiness

This physical and emotional need to take more and more of the drug in order to get high or just to feel normal is called addiction. Opium and the drugs that are made from opium ("opiates"), are extremely addictive. Users have to take more and more opiates to get the same high. Very quickly, they will feel sick if they do not take the drug. Sometimes even after just a few uses, opiate users have to take the drug just to feel normal.

Opium is the dried milk of a certain kind of poppy plant. Opium poppies grow well in warm, dry climates. The Sumerians, the inventors of writing and first city dwellers, were growing opium poppies (in what is now Iraq) as early as 3400 B.C. The Sumerians passed on what they knew about the opium poppy to other cultures.

By 1300 B.C., the Egyptians were growing and trading opium all over the Middle East and into Europe.

Around 400 B.C., Alexander the Great conquered much of the ancient world. Along with Greek thought, he brought opium to India and Persia. (The Persians lived where Iran is now.) The Persians and Indians started to grow huge quantities of opium poppies. About eight hundred years later, Arabs brought opium poppies to China as well.[2]

Opiates in Europe

During the Middle Ages, western Europe had very little contact with Asian and Middle Eastern cultures. So opium was not brought back to Europe until around 1600.

Up until this time, opium had only been eaten or made into a drink like tea. Portuguese sailors may have been the first to smoke opium.[3] Smoking any drug gets it into the brain much faster than eating or drinking it. This new method of using opium made users feel its effects much more quickly.

In the 1600s, the population of Europe was growing fast. Europeans began looking for more

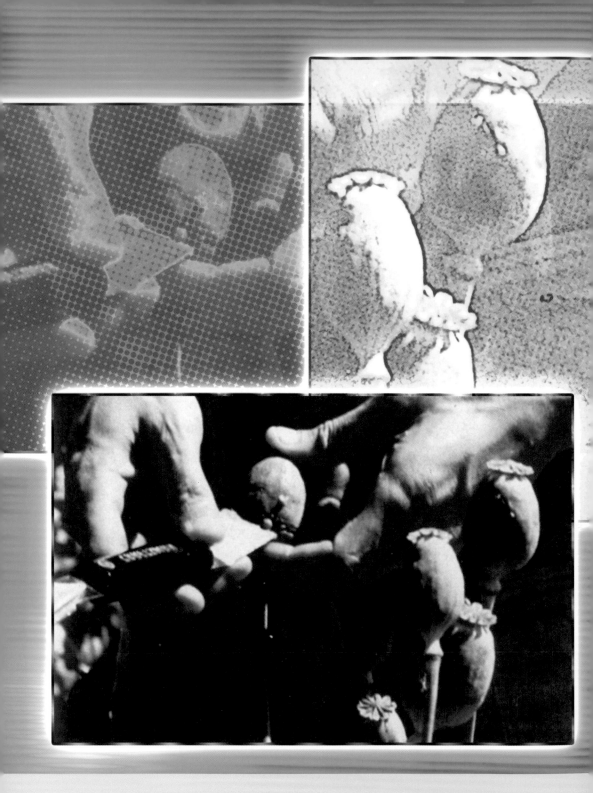

Farmers cut the pod to release the opium sap.

land. As they explored, they brought new things back to Europe. Soon Europeans wanted goods like spices, tea, and opium. In 1606, ships chartered by Queen Elizabeth I were told to buy the best Indian opium and bring it back to England.[4]

European merchants liked to trade opium. It weighed very little, and it did not rot. These two qualities made it ideal for sea travel. Plus, because it was hard to find in Europe, people were willing to pay a lot for it. Since opium is so addictive, users started to need it every day—like food. So the demand for it kept rising. Opium became as common in Europe as aspirin is today. Laudanum (a liquid mixture of opium, alcohol, and spices) could be bought at the corner store and could be found in most households.[5]

Opium also solved one of the biggest problems for European markets. Europeans wanted Chinese goods (especially tea), but the Chinese did not want European goods. To get China to trade with them, European merchants started bringing Indian opium to China.[6]

Opium addiction became such a problem in China that in 1729 the Chinese government made nonmedicinal opium illegal. But British and some American merchants did not want to give up such a good business. They kept selling it wherever they could along the coasts of China. Millions of Chinese became opium addicts. The Chinese government made all opium trade illegal in 1799. But opium was still widely used by Chinese addicts throughout the nineteenth century.

The Chinese emperor repeatedly asked the British government to stop British merchants from selling opium in China. The British parliament finally looked into the matter in 1830. Instead of stopping British opium sales in China, they concluded that it would not be good for Britain to lose such a valuable trade. The British finally went to war with China to force the government to allow them to legally sell opium to the Chinese.[7]

Opiates in the Americas

Opium became popular in the United States in the late 1800s. It was especially popular throughout the West. Immigrants from Asia, many of whom worked on building the railroads, brought the drug with them. Opium dens sprang up all over the United States. Opium dens were candlelit rooms that included beds where users could lie for days at a time in a drugged haze. They also

In the 1800s, opium dens sprang up across the United States.

became meeting places for gamblers, prostitutes, and criminals.[8]

During the nineteenth century, Americans could also buy morphine to ease their aches and pains. Morphine was the best pain reliever available at the time. As in Europe, it was common in most American homes. People took morphine for everything from headaches, diarrhea, and toothaches to serious illnesses like tuberculosis.

Morphine was particularly popular with middle-class women.[9] They used it not only for their own aches and pains, but they gave it to their children as well. Mothers who worked outside of their homes gave it to their children to keep them quiet during the day while they were gone. In crowded cities, mothers also gave it to their children at night to keep them from making noise that might bother their neighbors.[10]

In 1810, a new drug was created from opium. This new drug was able to quickly stop the pain of the worst injuries and surgeries. It was named morphine after the Greek god of dreams, Morpheus, because it left the patient totally numb and lying in a confused haze.[11]

By the 1850s, doctors in the United States could easily get morphine to stop their patients' pain. Morphine was a welcome tool for both doctors and patients. In fact, today morphine is still the drug used most often by hospitals to relieve terrible pain.[12]

It was not until the American Civil War that people in the United States started to notice how quickly users got addicted to morphine or opium. Both Confederate and Union soldiers were given opiates to ease the pain of the injuries they suffered in battle. But once they started taking opiates, they could not stop. So many soldiers

Raw morphine (top) is shaped into bricks before processing. Morphine was used, and still is, as a strong pain reliever in hospitals (bottom).

became addicted to opiates that, during the late nineteenth century, opiate addiction was called "the army disease."[13]

In 1898, Felix Hoffmann and Heinrich Dreser chemically purified morphine to make heroin.[14] They and other researchers at The Bayer Company in Germany were trying to make better pain relievers. (In the same year, they also made aspirin.)[15] The two biggest causes of death at that time were pneumonia and tuberculosis. Heroin relieved the coughs and chest pains caused by these diseases.[16] Heroin also seemed to cure morphine addiction because it lessened the pain users normally felt when they stopped taking morphine.

Heroin is much stronger than morphine. It is a more concentrated opiate from which more impurities have been removed. But when heroin was first available, doctors still thought it was much safer than morphine. Heroin seemed to be such a good drug that it was named after the German word for "heroic."[17] Doctors now know that heroin is one of the most addictive and dangerous drugs.

At the turn of the twentieth century, opiates were major goods in the world's economy. They

- In the 1970s, a dose of street heroin was 3–5% pure. Street heroin is now 20–65% pure, making the risk of addiction and overdose much greater.[18]
- From 1976 to 2002, more than 90% of twelfth graders disapproved of anyone even trying heroin.[19]

were traded as much as coffee and tea, and Americans could buy heroin at their local drugstores.[20] But in 1914, growing worry about the dangers of opiates led the United States Congress to pass the Harrison Act to limit the sale of opiates to those prescribed by doctors for diseases other than addiction.[21]

This change in public opinion and law helped stop two centuries of growth in world opiate production and use. World War II slowed the opiate trade even more. The tight security of ports during the war made smuggling opium more difficult. Unfortunately, soon after World War II ended, the use of opiates rose steadily again until the 1970s.[22]

Around the turn of the millennium, heroin use started growing again. There were two main reasons for the increased popularity of the drug. First, heroin producers began to be able to make

Opium dens were places people could go to smoke opium.

much purer heroin than they had been able to make before.

Most people would never try an illegal drug they have to inject into their bodies. Using a needle to inject a drug directly into a vein makes it seem much more dangerous. Shooting up also leaves ugly scars—track marks—on a junkie's skin that are obvious signs of heroin use.

But in the 1990s, users discovered they did not need to shoot up. They could get the same high by snorting the new, purer heroin.

In the 1990s, heroin use also grew because of the fashion industry. Photographers took pictures of models who were heroin addicts. They also purposely made other models look like heroin addicts. They posed very pale, skinny models in drugged dazes. Then fashion ads, most famously Calvin Klein's, used the same kinds of pictures to make it cool or "chic" to look like a junkie. It was only after the most famous heroin-chic photographer, Davide Sorrenti, died of a heroin overdose that heroin chic stopped being fashionable.[24]

The "Golden Triangle"
White Heroin Clearinghouses
in Southeast Asian Cities

Small amounts of opium harvested in Asia is used to make morphine. The rest is manufactured into illegal heroin. This heroin travels through the "golden triangle" before reaching the United States.

| Snorting heroin is a lot safer than injecting it. | VS. | Heroin users who do not shoot up still overdose. Overdose rates are rising because of the higher purity of today's street heroin. |

High purity heroin and heroin chic have drawn new, younger users who think heroin is not as dangerous as it used to be. But the opposite is true. Heroin is more dangerous than ever. Although newer users are not using needles, they are taking more heroin than junkies did in the past. Because they are using more of the drug, newer users are getting addicted to heroin even more quickly than users did in the past.[25]

Where Does Heroin Come From?

Heroin comes into the United States mainly from Southeast Asia, Southwest Asia, Mexico, and South America.

In the 1980s and early 1990s, most of the heroin in the United States came from Southeast Asia. But in 2001, Afghanistan banned heroin production. The governments of China and Iran have also worked very hard to stop the trade ("trafficking") of heroin in their countries. Finally, international cooperation between local law enforcement agencies put many of the biggest Southeast Asian heroin dealers in jail.[26]

But one of the bad effects of the war in Afghanistan after the September 11, 2001, al-Qaeda attack on the United States is that, in 2004, opium production sky-rocketed to higher than ever before. The war made times much harder for the Afghan people. They can make much more money growing opium poppies than other crops. So farmers who never grew opium before started growing it after the war. Afghanistan again produces more opium than any other country in the world. Plus, experts at the

Worldwide Production of Opium in 1998[27]	
Latin America (Colombia, Guatemala, Mexico)	2%
Southwest Asia (Afghanistan, Pakistan)	31%
Southeast Asia (Myanmar, Laos, Thailand)	66%

Street Names for Heroin

Balloon

Belushi (cocaine & heroin)

Brick Gum

Brown Sugar

Caballo (Spanish)

China White

Courage Pills

Crank

Dead On Arrival

Dr. Feelgood

Dyno/Dyno-pure

Foolish Powder (heroin; cocaine)

Gear

Galloping Horse

H

Hard Candy

Hell Dust

Hero

Horse

Joy Flakes

Junk

Mexican Black Tar

Mojo (cocaine; heroin)

Old Steve

Poison

Polvo

Racehorse Charlie (cocaine; heroin)

Rambo

Sack

Skag

Sleeper

Smack

T.N.T.

The Beast

White Nurse

Heroin Samples: Origin, Purities, and Prices[28]

	2000	2001	2002
Southeast Asian samples	5	7	10
Southeast Asian percent pure	22.0%	18.1%	23.9%
Southeast Asian price per milligram pure	$0.73	$0.56	$0.61
Southwest Asian samples	26	29	22
Southwest Asian percent pure	39.2%	26.5%	29.8%
Southwest Asian price per milligram pure	$0.55	$0.42	$0.75
Mexican samples	286	344	241
Mexican percent pure	24.9%	21.0%	27.3%
Mexican price per milligram pure	$0.93	$1.28	$0.70
South American samples	355	386	341
South American percent pure	51.3%	49.7%	46.0%
South American price per milligram pure	$0.72	$0.77	$0.72

United Nations think Afghanistan will try to keep producing even more opiates in the years to come.[29]

Colombian heroin has also become easier to get on the street. Colombian traffickers are very good at producing heroin inexpensively. Mexican drug traffickers are very good at smuggling heroin. Building on their strengths, Colombian and Mexican drug organizations have become partners.

The DEA is now worried that Afghan heroin traffickers will do the same. Or that Afghan heroin organizations could compete with South American drug organizations, making heroin cheaper and easier to get than ever before.[30]

Drug smugglers use lots of different ways to bring heroin into the United States. They hide it in shipments of legal goods like fruit, plastic bags, and straws. Some smugglers swallow little balloons filled with heroin and carry them past authorities in their stomachs.

In the past, smugglers moved heroin mainly on airplanes and boats. But now the Drug Enforcement Administration is seeing more heroin moved over ground. This method makes law enforcement officers' jobs harder because

Black Tar Heroin

Brown Heroin

China White Heroin

the United States has big borders that can be crossed at many unguarded places.

For example, large drug organizations are now buying land in California and Arizona along the border with Mexico. They dig tunnels under the border on that land and transport drugs through the tunnels. When these tunnels are found, the smugglers just start all over again somewhere else.

What Does Heroin Look Like?

Heroin comes in two basic forms. It can be made into a white or a brownish powder, and it can be made into a black, sticky paste that looks like tar.

In the western United States, smugglers usually bring in black tar heroin. Black tar heroin cannot be snorted, but it can be smoked. In the eastern United States, street heroin is usually white powder. This is the kind of heroin that can be snorted. Addicts can shoot up with both kinds of heroin.

CHAPTER FOUR

CHASING THE DRAGON

Michael used heroin for twelve years. When he finally kicked his habit, he stayed clean for five years other than one two-month relapse.[1]

Michael tried heroin for the first time on his twenty-sixth birthday. He had done other drugs, including cocaine. When his girlfriend gave him heroin that night, he was not sure he knew what it was. But he wanted to get higher. So he took the heroin.

"My first thought (and I think I said it out loud) was 'Where have you been all my life?'" He was talking about heroin, not his girlfriend.

"Most people get sick. You take a hit, your eyes roll back in your head, and you'll throw up whatever is in your stomach. Even a junkie who uses a much stronger grade of heroin than usual will get sick."

Unlike most users,[2] Michael did not get sick the first time he got high. He wished he had.

"When you take heroin, your body goes limp. You close your eyes. You have a total sense of well-being that's completely wrong. Bombs could be going off around you, and you wouldn't care. You don't have a sense of danger. You feel completely at peace. You have surrendered."

Michael found out the hard way how quickly a user can get addicted to heroin.

- In 2002, 3,668,000 people in the United States (aged twelve or older) were estimated to have used heroin at least once.[3]
- The Department of Health and Human Services estimated that in 2002 there were 166,000 current heroin users in the United States.[4]

"A high lasts about ninety minutes. After that, you're already looking for more. If you do heroin three days in a row and you don't take it on the fourth day, you'll start to twitch. I've never met anyone who's been able to use it [just when they wanted to]."

The next three years were just the beginning of Michael's addiction. He had a lot of responsibility as a very successful music producer, and he realized he could not do his job if he was using heroin. So he stopped using for a while.

"But every day I was sober I thought about getting high."

Then Michael and his girlfriend broke up. The breakup was very hard on him emotionally. So he went out to buy ("cop") some heroin.

"That's what happens. Something will happen to you physically, and then an emotional thing will happen. You snap and go cop."

That was when Michael's secret life of heroin use really started.

"You have to live a secret life. You cross from being a . . . get-it-done human to a professional liar who will say or do anything to get high. The part of your heart that wants to stay attached to your real friends goes to war with the part of you

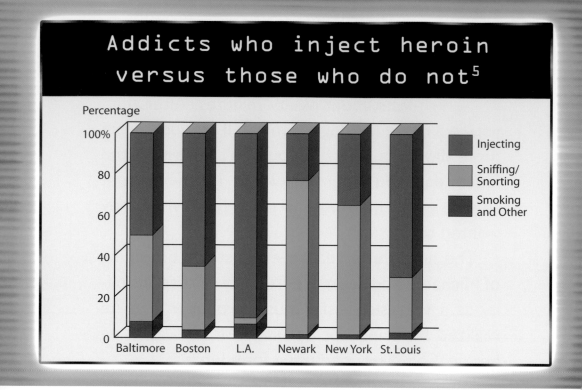

Addicts who inject heroin versus those who do not[5]

Percentage

Legend:
- Injecting
- Sniffing/Snorting
- Smoking and Other

Cities: Baltimore, Boston, L.A., Newark, New York, St. Louis

that's the addict. As your friends leave you because of the drugs, you have more stress and more pain, so you turn to the drugs more.

"You also become addicted to the danger. I was carrying a 357 magnum [handgun] and, at one point, a MAC-10 [semi-automatic assault gun]. There was next to no line I wouldn't cross.

"But underneath it all, you're a scared child who's putting up as many walls as possible to keep from feeling like a human. You're thinking, 'I don't want to feel anything. So let me do this to stop myself from feeling.'

"That's when things got really bad. I went through about three million dollars in four years.

All my houses. When I got finished, all I had was a bicycle.

"When you're all the way into the addiction, you're part of the walking dead. You don't even want to eat. It's so powerful that, when [you don't have it], you feel like you're missing an entire part of yourself. There's no hope. You're sure you can't get through a day without it.

"Heroin is the worst kind of cop out because it doesn't feel like it [is one]. It's the shortcut to feeling comfortable in your own skin.

"The first five or six times, you are so happy. I was always chasing that first time. You feel like the solution to your problem is that complete silence [of the high] that you never want to leave.

"You get to a point where no matter how much money you've got, you're not getting any higher. At the end of your cycle, you're just putting heroin into your body not to get sick. You spend more money and you do more drugs to feel nothing."

Michael was using forty bags of heroin a day at the height of his addiction. Most heroin addicts use about ten bags a day. Michael was using so much heroin that he had to buy as much as a heroin dealer. So when he got arrested, the judge did not believe that he was not dealing. Michael ended up in prison for a while on a felony drug charge.

He also almost died.

"I overdosed once. I turned blue. My friend stayed up with me all night, slapping me and feeding me coffee. Eventually, I woke up."

Michael tried to quit using heroin many times before he was successful. When junkies try to stop using heroin, they call it trying to "kick the habit." When they do it without taking any other drugs to help them through it, they call it going "cold turkey" because of the cold flashes that give them goose bumps all over their bodies.

"I kicked dope cold probably forty times.

"Withdrawal is like hell. You twitch and sneeze. Then you start coughing. Then the [muscle cramps] start. You're sick to your stomach. Your body is locked in a torture chamber. You sweat and have uncontrollable diarrhea. You won't sleep, and you'll shake. You can't eat or drink. Withdrawal is painful and horrible.

"Suicide goes along with withdrawal. If I'd had a plate glass window [in front of me], I would have jumped out of it."

In the years during which Michael tried to stop

Heroin Withdrawal Symptoms[b]

- **Cold flashes with goose bumps**
- **Body shakes**
- **Diarrhea**
- **Vomiting**
- **Itchy, clammy skin**

- **Restlessness**
- **Insomnia**
- **Muscle and bone pain**
- **Kicking movements**
- **Drug craving**

using heroin, he lived at three different drug treatment centers.

"The first time was for thirty days. The second time was for twenty-one days, and then they told me I could go. [I stayed clean] about a year collectively from those places."

But Michael kept trying. He eventually checked in to another treatment center.

"I was ready. I had no options. I was completely broke. My best friend had asked me to either leave his house (because it was too painful to watch me kill myself) or he would help me go to treatment. So I sold some Bob Marley posters I had and went in for two months.

"The chance of people making it out of rehab [clean] is about 10%, tops. But there is a way out. Narcotics Anonymous saved my life.

In 1997, a study of heroin addicts begun in 1962 found that:

- **nearly half the group had died**
- **the most common cause of death in the group (21.6%) was accidental poisoning or drug overdose**
- **20.7% of those still alive were actively using heroin**
- **during any given year of the study about 10% of the group was receiving treatment for heroin addiction**[7]

That's the only thing that worked. It's based on fundamental honesty ('to thine own self be true'). Most addicts aren't able to be honest with themselves, let alone others."

Michael made a deep commitment to changing his life.

"The first three years, I went to a meeting every day. If I wasn't in a place where I could go to a meeting, I could call my sponsor and talk for about an hour. I still go to meetings three to four times a week to stay focused on listening to others."

After seventeen years of battling heroin, Michael was full of hope. He was full of hope that

Heroin Use Health Risks [8]

- Addiction
- Inability to eat or properly digest food
- Loss of muscle mass and tone
- Paranoia
- Obsessive/compulsive behavior
- Depression
- Collapsed veins
- Infection of the lining and valves of the heart
- Abscesses (boils and other soft-tissue infections)
- Bacterial infections
- Cellulitis
- Liver disease
- Lung disease like pneumonia and tuberculosis
- Complications from depressed breathing
- Clogged blood vessels leading to the lungs, liver, kidneys, or brain.
- Spontaneous abortion
- Arthritis and other rheumatologic problems
- Infectious diseases including HIV and hepatitis
- Death

he had put his life back together and that he would stay clean.

But within six months of this interview, Michael died from a heroin overdose.

EXCERPTS FROM A JUNKIE'S SISTER'S DIARY

November 3rd[1]

I didn't get much sleep last night because of all the fighting. It seemed like Mom and Dad were yelling at Tommy forever. I feel a little bad because of what I did. But he put a knife to my throat and made me clean his room again.

It made me really mad.

I just kept thinking maybe I'd find something in his room to get him in trouble. Of course, I did. Dad put the needle that was in Tommy's drawer right on his dinner plate and told Tommy he should eat it if he liked his drugs so much.

I thought it would make me feel better, but it didn't.

February 23rd

Mom and Dad are talking about selling our country house. Five of the horses are missing. Tommy says he sold them to buy feed. But we all know it was for his drugs.

Dad did the usual and sent Tommy to his room halfway through dinner. He's grounded, but I heard him going out the window anyway. I can always hear him walking on the roof of the garage when he goes out at night.

I don't like to think about where he goes.

October 15th

Tommy got arrested again. Dad won't talk about it, so Mom went to get him. She had to pay a lot of money to get him out, so I guess I won't get to go back to sleepover camp this summer.

Mom said Tommy's in really big trouble. I asked what drug stuff the cops found on him. She said they didn't find any drugs this time. But they found Tommy sleeping under a stolen car with Dad's gun tucked in his jeans. Now he has to meet with a police officer every week.

Maybe he'll finally stop.

October 26th

I can't sleep again. The TV's on too loud. Tommy stays up all night watching it now. I guess he doesn't have any friends anymore.

He still says he didn't do anything that night with the gun. But sometimes, when he can't stop talking, he says the cops are going to find a way to say he did.

He's never been this way before. It's like he's freaking out or something. Every time he hears a noise, he looks around like they're coming for him.

And he found my new hiding place for my babysitting money.

Tools for using heroin.

Sometimes I hate him. It was almost better when he was always going out. Now he's home most of the time, but he just sits in front of the TV—all skinny and gross and staring.

December 7th

The cops came to the house and took Tommy away today. Mom and Dad couldn't get him out right away this time. It's all because of that night with the gun.

I really don't want to go to school tomorrow. Brian Corcoran's mom is one of the people who say Tommy robbed them. How am I going to face Brian and all the other kids?

December 11th

We got Tommy out on bail today. I guess that's good, except Mom said we're going to have to sell the store because it was so much money.

The police are saying Tommy did horrible things.

They're saying he put Dad's gun into a man's back and took all his money. Then they're saying he tried to steal Mrs. Corcoran's purse. But I guess at first she wouldn't give it to him. So they're saying Tommy shot the gun at her until she did.

Tommy says he didn't do any of it.

I want to believe him.

He finally admits he's been getting high again. But he says he would never do anything like robbing anyone.

EXCERPTS FROM
A JUNKIE'S SISTER'S DIARY

March 14th

Tommy's trial started today.

They brought him into the courtroom in handcuffs. He was all sweaty, shaky, and pale. I wonder if the jury knew it wasn't just because he was nervous. That's how he always looks if he hasn't been able to get high enough.

I hated sitting there in the front row behind him. It was so embarrassing the way everyone looked at us.

They charged him with two counts of armed robbery and one count of attempted murder. But the worst was when the prosecutor told the jury about how the police figured out what Tommy did. After listening to her, there's no way anyone could believe he didn't do it.

When they arrested Tommy that time with Dad's gun, he was sleeping under Mrs. Corcoran's car—probably because he had

MYTH		FACT
Heroin can be used without getting addicted.	VS.	Heroin is one of the most addictive drugs that exists.

gotten so high that he didn't want to do anything else.

The day before, Mrs. Corcoran told the police that a teenage boy had shot at her with a pistol that looked just like Dad's gun, stole her purse, and then stole her car. So the police showed Mrs. Corcoran Tommy's picture along with a bunch of other pictures of teenage boys. She picked Tommy out of the pictures and said he was the one who did it.

The other man, Mr. Rivera, was robbed in the same parking lot on the same day. So the police showed pictures to him, too, and he picked Tommy out of all of them.

Plus, a mall security guard saw Mrs. Corcoran being robbed. He picked Tommy's picture out of all the others just like Mrs. Corcoran and Mr. Rivera did.

Tommy still says it wasn't him, but even Mom doesn't believe him anymore.

March 18th

The jury came back today.

None of us were surprised when they said they had found Tommy guilty of all three crimes.

EXCERPTS FROM
A JUNKIE'S SISTER'S DIARY

It felt a lot like a dream. Tommy looked really scared. Mom almost seemed relieved.

And then the judge told us Tommy's punishment. For robbing Mrs. Corcoran, Tommy was sentenced to between fifteen and thirty years in prison. For robbing Mr. Rivera, he was sentenced to another fifteen to thirty years. Finally, for shooting at Mrs. Corcoran and stealing her car, he was sentenced to between twelve-and-a-half and twenty-five years.

All that time in jail seems like longer than one person's life could be. But Tommy's lawyer explained that it really means he'll be in jail for at least fifteen years.

I guess that's a lot better than what I thought at first—that he could be in jail for eighty-five years. But even if it's only fifteen years, he'll be really old by the time he gets out.

In 1991, 24% of federal prison inmates and 49% of state prison inmates said they were using alcohol or illegal drugs when they committed their crimes.[3]

CHAPTER FIVE

LYING, STEALING, AND TRYING TO CHEAT DEATH

Besides killing them, heroin addiction ruins users' lives. They spend all their money to buy heroin. They spend all their time looking for someone to sell them heroin. Usually they end up doing something criminal in order to keep getting more heroin. And heroin addiction does not just hurt addicts.

Heroin addiction is also very hard on addicts' families and friends. Up to 50 percent of all domestic violence is related to drugs or alcohol.[1]

Heroin often makes users cranky and argumentative even while they are high. This effect is partly because heroin makes users focus on their own thoughts. Everything else is a bother. The drug becomes a barrier between the user and the rest of the world. Other people and things are not nearly as interesting to junkies as what is going on inside their own heads. Most of the time they just want to be alone and get high. If they do want to interact with other people, they become know-it-alls who talk at people instead of to them.[2]

As addiction gets more serious, heroin users also resent anything that distracts them from thinking about how they are going to get their next high. Then, at some point, heroin stops getting them high at all. According to one ex-junkie, "You're constantly on the verge of a temper tantrum because . . . you never feel as good as you think you have a right to feel."[3]

Heroin users also have to spend a lot of time figuring out how to get more drugs. A heroin bag costs five or ten dollars, and an average addict

From 1986 through 2002, the Drug Enforcement Administration made 443,600 arrests related to the sale or possession of drugs.[4] Most of the crimes committed by drug users (especially heroin addicts) are not violent. Most drug users only commit crimes to get more money to buy drugs.[5]

needs ten bags a day. That means a heroin addict spends between $50 and $100 a day on heroin. Therefore, a heroin addict needs somewhere between $18,000 and $36,500 a year just for heroin.

At the same time, keeping a job gets harder and harder for a heroin user. Users often have to spend a lot of time buying heroin, or copping. Since heroin is illegal, they can never be sure how quickly they will be able to get more. They might not be able to find their regular dealer because he might be in jail. Or a dealer might take their money and give them something other than heroin. Because it can take so long to cop, it might be very late at night before they are able to get high. Then they might still be too high to hear the alarm clock when it rings in the morning. Or they might forget to set the alarm clock at all. Finally, they get fired for missing too many days of work.

But heroin addicts stop caring about work. Nothing is really important to heroin addicts other than heroin. They will find a way to get it. They will borrow as much money as they can. But eventually no one will lend them money because they cannot pay back what they have already borrowed. During the first year of heroin use, a typical addict loses about twenty-two pounds.[6]

Heroin addicts will also cut back on buying other things. They will buy less food in order to have more money for heroin. They will stop buying shampoo and deodorant in order to have more money for heroin. They will decide not to go out with their friends to save money for heroin. They will also stay away from their friends because they do not want to risk having to share their heroin.[7]

Addicts will also steal to get money for heroin. One of the worst ways in which heroin addicts hurt the people they love is by stealing from them. As an addiction gets worse, a junkie needs more and more heroin. But the more heroin they use, the harder it is for them to hold down a job. So they begin to do things that are illegal in order to get money. Most often, they steal. This stealing usually starts at home.

Drug use and abuse can lead to a court appearance.

U.S. Federal Penalties for Heroin Trafficking[a]

	100–999 Grams		1 Kilogram or More	
	Fine	**Imprisonment**	**Fine**	**Imprisonment**
First Offense	If an individual, not more than $2,000,000	Not less than 5 years in prison or more than 40 years	If an individual, not more than $4,000,000	Not less than 10 years or more than life
	If not an individual, not more than $5,000,000	If death or serious injury is involved, not less than 20 years or more than life	If not an individual, not more than $10,000,000	If death of serious injury is involved, not less than 20 years or more than life
Second Offense	If an individual, not more than $4,000,000	Not less than 10 years or more than life	If an individual, not more than $8,000,000	Not less than 20 years or more than life
	If not an individual, not more than $10,000,000	If death or serious injury is involved, not less than life	If not an individual, not more than $20,000,000	If death or serious injury is involved, not less than life
Two or More Prior Offenses		Not less than life.		Not less than life.

LYING, STEALING, AND TRYING TO CHEAT DEATH

Most recovering addicts admit that when it came to getting money for heroin, nothing was safe. They stole money from their parents' wallets and businesses. They sold family heirlooms. They stole from children's piggy banks. They sold healthy animals to slaughterhouses. In the words of one ex-addict, "A junkie is alone, and everyone to him is a target to be cheated, robbed, and deceived."[9] Drug dealers are more likely to carry guns than other serious juvenile delinquents.[10]

* * *

Tommy was released from prison after serving fifteen years of his sentence. But like most recovering addicts, he could not stay clean. Two years later, he died of a heroin overdose in his bathroom. He had not even taken his coat off before he put the needle in his arm.

CHAPTER SIX

TRYING TO KICK THE HEROIN HABIT

The Goodwill Rescue Mission in Newark, New Jersey, has ninety beds. Those beds are for men who are addicted to drugs or alcohol. Those ninety beds are full every night.

Ken and Kathy work at the Rescue Mission.[1] They help people stop abusing drugs and alcohol.

"The reality is that addiction is very much physical as well as mental." Ken knows what he is talking about. When he first came to the Rescue Mission, it was not to work. It was to get help for his alcohol addiction. Kathy was one of the people who helped him.

Ken and Kathy also work with heroin addicts. Heroin treatment starts with getting the drug out of the heroin user's body. That is a very painful process.

When a heroin user stops using the drug, he or she will usually shake and vomit as well as have cold flashes, muscle and bone aches, and diarrhea.[2] Kathy has seen people go through all these things.

MYTH

Heroin is just an inner-city problem.

FACT

Heroin is a popular suburban drug. It just is not as noticeable in the suburbs because kids with large allowances do not have to rob anyone to get money to buy heroin. They also have privacy to use heroin at home. These same kids get noticed as heroin addicts only when they end up with no money in the inner city trying to get more heroin.

"Heroin," Kathy explains, "is such a slavery. Trying to get off it alone doesn't work."

How sick a junkie feels when he or she stops taking heroin depends on three things:

- how much heroin he or she has been taking
- how healthy he or she is
- how fast he or she stops taking heroin

Doctors can give heroin addicts other drugs to help them stop using heroin. These drugs (methadone, LAAM, naltrexone, and buprenorphine) keep addicts from feeling as terrible as they should while their bodies get used to not having heroin. The addicts do not get sick. But they are not asleep either. So they can still do normal things like driving a car or going to work or school.[3]

Although it only takes about twenty-four hours for heroin to leave the body and about one week for all traces of it to be gone, it takes a lot longer for most addicts to stop wanting more of it. So they could need to take a treatment drug for years. By then, they are addicted to the treatment drug. To get an addict off a treatment drug, a doctor gives them less and less of it each time until they can feel normal without it.[4]

But addicts have to want to get off drugs. Ken

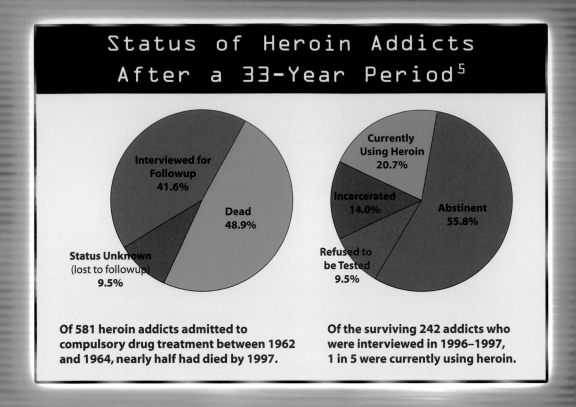

Status of Heroin Addicts After a 33-Year Period[5]

Interviewed for Followup
41.6%

Dead
48.9%

Status Unknown
(lost to followup)
9.5%

Currently Using Heroin
20.7%

Incarcerated
14.0%

Abstinent
55.8%

Refused to be Tested
9.5%

Of 581 heroin addicts admitted to compulsory drug treatment between 1962 and 1964, nearly half had died by 1997.

Of the surviving 242 addicts who were interviewed in 1996–1997, 1 in 5 were currently using heroin.

points out that people who are using methadone might still be using heroin at the same time. They sell the methadone their doctors give them to make money to buy heroin.[6] Ken explains, "Methadone has a great street value." Since methadone stops the symptoms of heroin withdrawal, heroin addicts who cannot find a heroin dealer will buy methadone instead.

Treatment drugs can work. But if an addict does not want to stop using heroin, treatment drugs will not make him or her stop. He or she might just end up being addicted to the treatment drug.[7]

Or an addict may not be able to get treatment drugs. Most of the heroin addicts Ken and Kathy work with cannot afford to pay for treatment drugs. Ken's experience helping drug addicts has led him to the same conclusions that Michael came to because of heroin.

"Drug addiction will certainly lead you to poverty," Ken says. "I've seen people with the most end up in the same place as people with the least."

Even if they can afford treatment drugs, there are more people who need them than there are drug treatment programs. So most people have to kick heroin without the help of treatment drugs.

Kathy explains, "We make them as comfortable as possible. The key thing is to help them understand that the difficult detox will be brief, and they'll get over it."

There is also more to being addicted to heroin than just the physical symptoms. Addiction is a feeling, too. Junkies keep hoping that using it again will make them feel as good as it did the first time they used it. Even though they know it never will, they still keep hoping it might. Heroin addicts call that "chasing the dragon."

Drugs Found in Tommy's Body After His Heroin Overdose

Besides opiates, the medical examiner reported that he also found the following drugs in Tommy's body:

- **Acetaminophen (Tylenol)**
- **Methadone (a heroin treatment drug)**
- **Hydrocodone (another opiate)**

All of Tommy's organs were healthy. His heart stopped beating because he took too large a dose of heroin.

Addicts, doctors, and drug abuse counselors all agree that once an addict gets heroin out of his or her body, there still is a long way to go to recover.[8]

The program at the Newark Rescue Mission lasts for at least nine months. During that time, addicts live at the Rescue Mission. The first thirty days are the hardest.

Ken is hopeful but realistic. "If they get past the blackout period, they might finish."

So is Kathy. "The main objective when someone starts a twenty-eight-day program is to teach them that twenty-eight days isn't enough."

During the blackout period, workers like Ken

and Kathy keep the people in their program constantly busy. And they focus on a lot more than addiction. They help with all the things that might make the addict vulnerable to addiction in the future.

Both Ken and Kathy think it is important to help addicts physically, emotionally, mentally, and spiritually. So their program starts with things as basic as making sure that people are eating a good, balanced diet. This is part of replacing addiction habits with habits that help keep the recovering addict clean and healthy.[9]

Their program, like most treatment programs, includes lots of classes for their clients. There are classes on how to read and how to use computers. There are classes on how to manage money and to help people finish high school or get better jobs.

Their program also includes lots of counseling. Counseling is important because drug abuse is

In 2000, only 27% of opiate addicts who were not living at treatment centers finished getting treatment.[10] Heroin treatment is most successful when the addict lives at the treatment center for at least three to six months.[11]

often related to other problems. Lack of education, lack of money, bad relationships, sadness, or worry can all drive people to drugs. Most people use drugs to stop the emotional pain that these problems cause them.

But if the thoughts that led a junkie to addiction can be changed, the behavior of addiction might change. So counselors help addicts talk about their problems in order to help them stop feeling the pain that made them start taking drugs. They also help addicts become part of a community in which they learn to respect and care for other people.[13]

Addicts also usually need help with other problems they have that could cause them to return to addictive behaviors. They might need legal help because their addiction led them to do something criminal. Their addiction might have left them with other serious health problems. Or they might just need to get a driver's license so they can travel to and from a job.

Finally, both Ken and Kathy share their spiritual faith with their clients.

Kathy explains, "People are so laden down with guilt and regret. The cure for that is forgiveness."

Even with all these treatments, it is very hard for addicts to stop using heroin for good. Like Michael and Tommy, most addicts who have stopped using heroin start using it again at some point. One study found that 25 percent of heroin addicts who had stopped using the drug for as long as fifteen years still relapsed into using it again.[14]

The beginning of that downhill slide is not as dramatic as one might think. It usually happens little by little. The addict stops spending time with his or her support group. That could be his or her family, friends, other recovering addicts, or some other support group. These people help an addict deal with everyday problems. Without the support of those people, an addict can start trying to stop the pain of their problems with drugs again.

Ken explains that then heroin is even more dangerous. "The longer they've been clean, the

Between 1993 and 1999, the number of people who entered treatment centers for heroin addiction rose between 100% and 200% in seventeen states.[15]

Top Ten Reasons
Not to Use Heroin

10. A junkie can never use enough heroin to satisfy his or her cravings for it.

9. Heroin users look awful. Because they stop eating, sleeping, and doing other things to take care of themselves, they get pale and skinny with big, dark circles around their eyes.

8. Heroin users do not want to be with other people. They just want to use heroin. So they shut themselves off from their family and friends.

7. Getting off heroin is incredibly painful. Withdrawal symptoms include cold sweats, body shakes, vomiting, muscle and bone pain, goose bumps, and itchy, clammy skin.

6. No matter how much money heroin addicts have, they never have enough to buy as much heroin as they want.

5. After just a few uses, heroin stops making junkies feel high. But they have to keep using heroin just so they do not feel sick.

4. Heroin addicts do not do anything else with their lives other than copping and getting high.

3. Junkies are at high risk for being infected with HIV or Hepatitis B. These diseases are both often fatal.

2. A lot of heroin addicts end up in prison.

1. Heroin kills.

more the danger of overdosing. The tolerance isn't there, so it's more of a shock to the body."

While heroin addiction is very hard to break, it can be done. Studies have also shown that addicts who stopped using heroin for more than five years are less likely to start again.[16]

Kathy believes, "One of the key elements is putting off the old. But you have to replace it with a good new habit. You have to replace it with something that will build you up instead of breaking you down. Learning and practicing new habits is a lifetime thing."

Kathy gets to see people practicing new habits every day when she looks around at her staff at the Rescue Mission. Half of them did not first come to the Rescue Mission as workers. They came as addicts.

GLOSSARY

addiction—Physical and emotional need for a habit-forming substance.

chasing the dragon—Using more and more heroin to try to feel the same way it felt the first time.

copping—Buying heroin.

DEA—Drug Enforcement Administration.

dependence—A very strong need for something. Someone who has a dependence on alcohol cannot stop himself from drinking it.

depressed—To feel sad and gloomy; to lack any enthusiasm.

endorphin—A chemical that is naturally in the brain to relieve pain when necessary and to make the body feel good.

felony—A serious crime, often punishable by time in jail.

junkie—A heroin addict.

juvenile delinquent—Someone eighteen or younger who commits crimes.

laudanum—A liquid mixture of opium, alcohol, and spices.

opiate—Any drug that is made from opium.

overdose—To take more of a drug than the body can recover from by itself.

pneumonia—A serious lung infection that can be fatal.

rehabilitation—To restore someone to good health and a useful life through therapy and education.

snort—To inhale through the nose.

substance abuse—Overusing or being a dependent on an addictive substance, such as alcohol or a drug.

tolerance—The ability/need to take increasing amounts of substance without ill effects.

track marks—Needle scars from injecting drugs.

trafficking—To buy or sell illegal goods.

tuberculosis—A disease in which bacteria causes tumors to form around infections in the organs.

withdrawal—A variety of symptoms that occur after use of an addictive drug is reduced or stopped.

CHAPTER NOTES

Chapter 1. Busted

1. Personal phone interview with Drug Enforcement Administration agent Ed Childress, January 30, 2004. Minor details and/or names have been changed in all interview material to protect identities.
2. National Institute on Drug Abuse, "Monitoring the Future: National Survey Results on Adolescent Drug Use, Overview of Key Findings," 2003, <http://www.monitoringthefuture.org/pubs/monographs/overview2003.pdf> (December 12, 2004).
3. Ibid.

Chapter 2. From Flower to Fatal

1. Tom Cornwath and Ian Smith, *Heroin Century* (London: Routledge, 2002), p. 23.
2. *Frontline*, "The Opium Kings," *Transforming Opium Poppies into Heroin*, 1998, <http://www.pbs.org/wgbh/pages/frontline/shows/heroin/transform/> (November 21, 2003).
3. Ibid.
4. Narcanon Southern California, "Heroin Addiction," *Heroin Effects*, 2003, <http://www.heroinaddiction2.com/heroin-effects.htm> (November 21, 2003).

5. J. J. Jenkins, R. M. Keenan, J. E. Henninfield, and E. J. Cone, "Pharmacokinetics and Pharmacodynamics of Smoked Heroin," *Journal of Analytical Toxicology*, 18, 1994, pp. 317–330; Substance Abuse and Mental Health Services Administration, "The DASIS Report: Heroin Treatment Admissions Increase: 1993–1999," 2003, <http://oas.samhsa.gov/2k2/HeroinTX/HeroinTX.htm> (November 21, 2003).

6. *Frontline*, "The Opium Kings," *Heroin in the Brain*, 1998, <http://pbs.org/wgbh/pages/frontline/shows/heroin/brain/> (November 21, 2003).

7. Patrick Zickler, "33-Year Study Finds Lifelong, Lethal Consequences of Heroin Addiction," 2003, <http://www.heroinaddiction2.com/heroin-research-information.htm> (November 21, 2003).

8. Drug Abuse Warning Network, Preliminary Estimates of Drug-Related Emergency Department Episodes, 1993, (Substance Abuse and Mental Health Administration, 1994).

9. Narcanon Southern California, "Heroin Addiction," *Heroin Effects*, 2003, <http://www.heroinaddiction2.com/heroin-effects.htm> (November 21, 2003).

10. Tom Field, *Escaping the Dragon* (London: Unwin Paperbacks, 1985), p. 46.

11. Narcanon Southern California, "Heroin Addiction," *Heroin Effects*, 2003, <http://www.heroinaddiction2.com/heroin-effects.htm> (November 21, 2003).

12. Drug Enforcement Administration, "Briefs and Background," *Heroin Factsheet*, 2003, <http://www.dea.gov/concern/heroin_factsheet.html> (November 21, 2003).

13. Narconon Southern California, "Heroin Addiction," *Heroin Effects*, 2003, <http://www.heroinaddiction2.com/heroin-effect.htm> (November 21, 2003).

Chapter 3. Putting Out Fires With Gasoline

1. National Institute on Drug Abuse, "InfoFacts," Heroin, 2003, <http://www.nida.nih.gov/Infofax/heroin.html> (November 21, 2003); Narcanon, "Heroin Addition," *Heroin Information*, <http://www.heroinaddiction2.com/heroin-information.htm> (November 21, 2003); Ann Marlowe, *How to Stop Time: Heroin from A to Z* (New York: Anchor Books, 2000).

2. *Frontline*, "The Opium Kings," *Transforming Opium Poppies into Heroin*, 1998, <http://www.pbs.org/wgbh/pages/frontline/shows/heroin/transform/> (November 21, 2003).

3. *Frontline*, "The Opium Kings," *Heroin in the Brain*, 1998, <http://pbs.org/wgbh/pages/frontline/shows/heroin/brain/> (November 21, 2003).

4. In the Know Zone, "Heroin," *History*, 2003, <http://www.intheknowzone.com/heroin/history.htm> (November 21, 2003).

5. Tom Cornwath and Ian Smith, *Heroin Century* (London: Routledge, 2002), p. 6.

6. R. R. Colton and Joel Palmer, *A History of the Modern World*, seventh ed. (New York: McGraw-Hill, Inc., 1992), p. 675.

7. Justine Picardie and Dorothy Wade, *Heroin: Chasing the Dragon* (Harmondsworth, U.K.: Penguin Books Ltd., 1985), p. 120.

8. David T. Courtwright, *Dark Paradise: A History of Opiate Addiction in America* (Cambridge: Harvard University Press, 2001), pp. 63–64, 69–77.

9. Ibid., pp. 40–41.

10. Cornwath and Smith, p. 6.

11. David F. Musto, "The Origins of Heroin" in *One Hundred Years of Heroin*, ed. David F. Musto (Westport, Conn.: Auburn House, 2002), p. xiii; Heroin Awareness Foundation, "History of Heroin," 2003, <http://www.heroinhelp.net/history_of_heroin.htm> (November 21, 2003).

12. In the Know Zone, "Heroin," *History*, 2003, <http://www.intheknowzone.com/heroin/history.htm> (November 21, 2003).

13. Courtwright, pp. 54–55.

14. Musto, p. xiv.

15. Cornwath and Smith, p. 17.

16. David T. Courtwright, "The Roads to H: The Emergence of the American Heroin Complex, 1898–1956," in *One Hundred Years of Heroin*, ed.

David F. Musto (Westport, Conn.: Auburn House, 2002), p. 4.

17. In the Know Zone, "Heroin," *History*, 2003, <http://www.intheknowzone.com/heroin/history.htm> (November 21, 2003).

18. Personal phone interview with Drug Enforcement Administration agent Ed Childress, January 30, 2004.

19. Monitoring the Future, "National Survey Results on Drug Use, 1975–2002," *2002 Data From In-School Surveys of 8th, 10th, and 12th Grade Students*, 2003, <http://monitoringthefuture.org/data/02data/pr02t11.pdf> (November 21, 2003).

20. David T. Courtwright, "The Roads to H: The Emergence of the American Heroin Complex, 1898–1956," in *One Hundred Years of Heroin*, ed. David F. Musto (Westport, Conn.: Auburn House, 2002), p. 7.

21. Leo Smits, *Getting Off: an Anthropological Analysis of Heroin Users*, vol. 12 of Papers on European and Mediterranean Societies (Amsterdam: University of Amsterdam, 1980), p. 12.

22. David T. Courtwright, *Dark Paradise: A History of Opiate Addiction in America*, pp. 147–149; Heroin Awareness Foundation, "History of Heroin," 2003, <http://www.heroinhelp.net/history_of_heroin.htm> (November 21, 2003).

23. U.S. Drug Enforcement Administration Resources,

"Intelligence Reports," *Drug Trafficking in the United States*, 2003, <http://www.dea.gov/pubs/intel/01020/index.html#heroin> (November 21, 2003).

24. Amy M. Spindler, "A Death Tarnishes Fashion's Heroin Look," *New York Times*, May 20, 1997, <http://www.nytimes.com/library/style/heroin-fashion.html> (August 25, 2004).

25. U.S. Drug Enforcement Administration Resources, "Intelligence Reports," *Drug Trafficking in the United States*, 2003, <http://www.dea.gov/pubs/intel/01020/index.html#heroin> (November 21, 2003); U.S. Drug Enforcement Administration, "Major Heroin Organization Dismantled from the Source in Colombia to the Streets of Philadelphia," press release, May 20, 2003, <http://www.dea.gov/pubs/states/newsreel/phila052003.html> (November 21, 2003).

26. United Nations Office on Drugs and Crime, "Global Illicit Drug Trends," 2003, pp. 52–53, 56–57, 61.

27. U.S. Central Intelligence Agency, "Heroin Movement Worldwide," 1998, <http://www.cia.gov/di/products/cncweb/homt.htm> (December 15, 2004).

28. U.S. Drug Enforcement Administration Resources, "Intelligence Reports," *Drug Trafficking in the United States*, 2003, <http://www.dea.gov/pubs/intel/01020/index.html#heroin> (November 21, 2003).

29. United Nations Office on Drugs and Crime, "Afghanistan Opium Survey 2004," 2004, <http://www.unodc.org/unodc/en/world_drug_report.html> (December 12, 2004); Jerry Seper, "Afghanistan leads again in heroin production," *Washington Times*, 2003, <http://www.washtimes.com/national/20030811-100220-8928r.htm> (December 12, 2004); Associated Press, "U.N.: Afghan poppies driving worldwide opium production," 2004, <http://www.usatoday.com/news/health/2004-06-25_un-opium_x.htm> (December 12, 2004).

30. Jerry Seper, "Afghanistan leads again in heroin production," *Washington Times*, 2003, <http://www.washtimes.com/national/20030811-100220-8928r.htm> (December 12, 2004).

Chapter 4. Chasing the Dragon

1. Personal phone interview with Michael Kough, November 28, 2003.

2. Alcohol, Drug Abuse, and Mental Health Administration, *Epidemiology of Heroin: 1964–1984*, (Washington, D.C., U.S. Department of Health and Human Services, 1985), p. 6.

3. Substance Abuse and Mental Health Services Administration, Office of Applied Studies, "2002 National Survey on Drug Use & Health," 2003, <http://www.samhsa.gov/oas/nhsda/2k2nsduh/

html/Sect1peTabs1to110.htm#tab1.1a>
(November 21, 2003).

4. Substance Abuse and Mental Health Services Administration, Office of Applied Studies, "2002 National Survey on Drug Use & Health," *Highlights of Findings*, 2003 <http://www. samhsa.gov/oas/nhsda/2k2nsduh/Overview/ 2k2Overview.htm#highlights> (November 21, 2003).

5. National Institute on Drug Abuse, "Research Report Series—Heroin Abuse and Addiction," 2003, <http://www.drugabuse.gov/ResearchReports/ Heroin/heroin2.html#scope> (November 21, 2003).

6. National Institute on Drug Abuse, "InfoFacts," *Heroin*, 2003, <www.nida.nih.gov/Infofax/heroin. html> (November 21, 2003); Narcanon Southern California, "Heroin Addiction," *Heroin Effects*, 2003, <http://www.heroinaddiction2. com/heroin-information.htm> (November 21, 2003).

7. Patrick Zickler, "33-Year Study Finds Lifelong, Lethal Consequences of Heroin Addiction," 2003, <http://www.heroinaddiction2.com/heroin-research-information.htm> (November 21, 2003).

8. National Institute on Drug Abuse, "Research Reports," *Heroin Abuse and Addiction*, 2003, <http://165.112.78.61/ResearchReports/heroin/ heroin3.html> (November 21, 2003); National

Institute on Drug Abuse, "InfoFacts," *Heroin*, 2003, <www.nida.nih.gov/Infofax/heroin.html> (November 21, 2003); Narcanon Southern California, "Heroin Addiction," *Heroin Effects*, 2003, <http://www.heroinaddiction2.com/heroin-information.htm> (November 21, 2003).

Excerpts From a Junkie's Sister's Diary

1. All diary entries are based on personal interview with Maria Marterra, Jersey City, New Jersey, March 7, 2003.
2. Monitoring the Future, "National Survey Results on Drug Use, 1975–2002," *2002 Data From In-School Surveys of 8th, 10th, and 12th Grade Students*, 2003, <http://monitoringthefuture.org/data/02data/pr02t2.pdf> (November 21, 2003).
3. "Drug Abuse Cost to Society Set at $97.7 Billion, Continuing Steady Increase Since 1975," *NIDA Notes*, 1998, <http://www.drugabuse.gov/nida_notes/nnvol13n4/abusecosts.html> (November 21, 2003).

Chapter 5. Lying, Stealing, and Trying to Cheat Death

1. Bureau of Justice Statistics, "Drugs and Crime Facts," *Drug Use and Crime*, 2004, <http://www.

ojp.usdoj.gov/bjs/dcf/duc.htm> (December 15, 2004).

2. Tom Field, *Escaping the Dragon* (London: Unwin Paperbacks, 1985), pp. 50–51.

3. Ann Marlowe, *How to Stop Time: Heroin from A to Z* (New York: Anchor Books, 2000), p. 184.

4. U.S. Drug Enforcement Administration, "Statistics," 2003, <http://www.dea.gov/statisticsp.html> (November 21, 2003).

5. National Institute on Drug Abuse, "The Economic Costs of Alcohol and Drug Abuse in the United States—1992," 2002, <http://www.drugabuse.gov/economiccosts/chapter6.html> (November 21, 2003).

6. Narcanon Southern California, "Heroin Addiction," *Heroin Addict*, 2003, <http://www.heroinaddiction2.com/heroin-information.htm> (November 21, 2003).

7. Tam Stewart, *The Heroin Users* (London: Pandora, 1987), pp. 65–101.

8. U.S. Drug Enforcement Administration, "Federal Trafficking Penalties," 2003, <http://www.dea.gov/agency/penalties.htm> (November 21, 2003).

9. Field, pp. 66–67.

10. Substance Abuse and Mental Health Services Administration, "Prevention Pathways," n.d., <http://www.preventionpathways.samhsa.gov/res-fact-yviolence.htm> (December 15, 2004).

Chapter 6. Trying to Kick the Heroin Habit

1. Personal phone interview with Kathy Smookler, February 11, 2004; Personal phone interview with Rev. Ken Thomas, February 11, 2004.

2. Tam Stewart, *The Heroin Users* (London: Pandora, 1987), pp. 154–160; Mary Kenny, *Death by Heroin, Recovery by Hope* (Dublin: New Island, 1999), p. 135.

3. National Institute on Drug Abuse, Research Report Series, "Heroin Abuse and Addiction," *What Are the Treatments for Heroin Addiction*, 2003, <http://www.nida.nih.gov/ResearchReports/ heroin/heroin5.html#treatment> (November 21, 2003); John C. Ball and Alan Ross, *The Effectiveness of Methadone Maintenance Treatment: Patients, Programs, Services, and Outcomes* (New York: Springer-Verlag, 1991), passim; Jack D. Blaine, ed., *Buprenorphine: an Alternative Treatment for Opioid Dependence* (Rockville: U.S. Department of Health and Human Services, Public Health Service, Alcohol, Drug Abuse, and Mental Health Administration, National Institute on Drug Abuse, 1992), passim.

4. Kenny, p. 142.

5. Patrick Zickler, "33-Year Study Finds Lifelong, Lethal Consequences of Heroin Addiction," n.d., <http://www.heroinaddiction2.com/heroin-

research-information.htm> (November 21, 2003).

6. Tom Field, *Escaping the Dragon* (London: Unwin Paperbacks, 1985), p. 73; Stewart, p. 188.

7. Kenny, p. 140.

8. Stewart, p. 160; Kenny, p. 136.

9. James G. Barber, *Social Work with Addictions* (London: MacMillan, 1995), pp. 92–115, 122–140; Liz Cutland, *Kick Heroin: A Guide for Those concerned with Addicts* (London: Sky Books, 1985), pp. 92, 94–95.

10. Substance Abuse and Mental Health Services Administration, Office of Applied Studies, "The DASIS Report: Discharges from Outpatient Treatment, 2000," *Highlights*, 2003, <http://www.oas.samhsa.gov/2k3/outpatientDischarges/outpatientDischarges.cfm> (November 21, 2003).

11. National Institute on Drug Abuse, Research Report Series, "Heroin Abuse and Addiction," *What Are the Treatments for Heroin Addiction*, 2003, <http://www.nida.nih.gov/ResearchReports/heroin/heroin5.html#treatment> (November 21, 2003).

12. United Nations Office on Drugs and Crime, "Global Illicit Drug Trends," 2003, p. 7.

13. John J. Benshoff and Timothy P. Janikowski, *The Rehabilitation Model of Substance Abuse Counseling* (Belmont: Wadsworth, 2000), pp. 125–130.

14. Y-I. Hser, V. Hoffman, C. E. Grella, and M. D.

Anglin, "A 33-Year Follow-Up of Narcotics Addicts," *Archives of General Psychiatry*, 58, May 2001, p. 507.

15. Substance Abuse and Mental Health Services Administration, "The DASIS Report: Heroin Treatment Admissions Increase: 1993–1999," *Highlights*, 2003, <http://www.oas.samhsa.gov/2k2/HeroinTX/HeroinTX.cfm> (November 21, 2003).

16. Hser, et al., p. 507.

FURTHER READING

Cobb, Allan J. *Heroin and Your Veins: The Incredibly Disgusting Story*. New York: Rosen Central, 2000.

Connolly, Sean. *Heroin*. Chicago: Heinemann Library, 2001.

Ferreiro, Carmen. *Heroin*. Philadelphia, Penn.: Chelsea House Publishers, 2003.

Graves, Bonnie. *Drug Use and Abuse*. Mankato, Minn.: LifeMatters, 2000.

Howard, Todd. *Heroin*. San Diego, Calif.: Lucent, 2003.

Hyde, Margaret O. and John F. Setaro. *Drugs 101: An Overview for Teens*. Brookfield, Conn.: Twenty-First Century Books, 2003.

Papa, Susan. *Addiction*. Woodbridge, Conn.: Blackbirch Press, 2001.

Weintraub, Aileen. *Heroin*. Berkeley Heights, N. J.: Enslow Publishers, Inc., 2005.

Westcott, Patsy. *Why Do People Take Drugs?* Austin, Tex.: Raintree Steck-Vaughn Publishers, 2001.

INTERNET ADDRESSES

Does Your Friend Have an Alcohol or Other Drug Problem: A Guide for Teens

<http://www.health.org/govpubs/phd688>

This site from the U.S. Department of Health and Human Services offers this publication to help if you know someone who may have an alcohol or drug problem.

Mind Over Matter

<http://www.nida.nih.gov/MOM/MOMIndex.html>

Click on "Opiates" to learn what happens to the brain when opiates are taken. This site is from the National Institute on Drug Abuse and the National Institutes of Health.

INDEX